MW00794938

Guatemalan Spanish

Speak like a Native!

LEE JAMISON

Visit us at www.gringoguide200.com

PHOTO CREDITS

To my mother Janice,
for all your guidance in the early years.

gringoguide200

Guatemalan Spanish

ACKNOWLEDGEMENTS

A WORK of this sort can never be accomplished without the help of many contributors. Foremost of all, I thank my wife Moraima for her continued encouragement and suggestions. Thanks as well to Marco and Alicia Casillas and Jason and Emily Provchy for the office space provided me during the preparation of this volume. Much gratitude goes also to Jorge Urrutia, Danny Flores, Christopher Rasicci, and Alfredo Mazariegos—all native speakers—for clearing up details about some of Guatemala's most beautiful traditional sayings. And, lastly, I am indebted to the people of Guatemala, for their painstaking patience with all of us foreigners who have learned your most delightful version of Spanish one explanation at a time.

gringoguide2OO

Guatemalan Spanish

TABLE OF CONTENTS

Guatemalan Spanish

INTRODUCTION

A N international organization had recently merged personnel from several Latin American countries. A Mexican explained to a group of Guatemalans that there were still a lot of holes, or **huecos,** in the department. The listeners erupted in laughter. In their Spanish, **huecos** is slang for *homosexuals.*

In another conversation someone said that he had crashed his car, or **coche.** But again came giggles from the other end. In Guatemala, **coches** are *pigs,* not *cars.* Have you crashed yours lately?

All piggishness aside, in the global marketplace just knowing Spanish is not enough. Learning the country-specific peculiarities of the language is the only way to avoid potentially costly misunderstandings. The goal of the *GringoGuide200* series of books is to help you to do just that. Imitating regional speech dignifies the locals.

And even though to them you are the foreigner, some may well come to regard you as one of the family. Your efforts will definitely be rewarded—many times over!

Are you thinking of visiting Guatemala or are you living there now? Do you have family there or from there? Or are you just a language buff? Whatever the case, we urge you: Join the linguistic party! Instead of stubbornly clinging to phrasebook Spanish, have an open mind! Embrace those new but yet unfamiliar words and phrases! The more local words, phrases, and sayings you begin to use in your daily vocabulary, the more you will fit in.

One size does not fit all

The avalanche of books on Spanish has left us knee deep in a language that no one actually speaks. Real Hispanics don't read out of phrasebooks. To them they are as stale as week-old bread. Everyday speech is full of color that is country-specific. Consider:

The generic word for "white" is **blanco.** But when describing a light-skinned person, Mexicans will instinctively use the term **güero.** In El Salvador, Nicaragua and Honduras they say **chele.** In Panama it's **fulo,** but as you will see in this volume, the residents of the "Land of Eternal Spring" will invariably speak of a **canche.** (See page 151.)

That's where the *GringoGuide200* series comes in. In this volume, we don't teach you Spanish; we teach you to make your Spanish *more Guatemalan*, to speak like a native. How? We have made an effort to identify 200 words and phrases that are endemic to the country. We cannot dogmatically state that they are only used in Guatemala. Immigration agents don't detain words at the border, as if they had need of passports. Nevertheless, *as a group* they are like a fingerprint that unequivocally identifies the Spanish of any given country. For any Guatemalan who finds himself far from his native land, these words will be music to his hears.

Why 200?

One common saying is **El que mucho abarca, poco aprieta.** It literally means: *He who tries to encompass a lot, squeezes a little.* The idea is that we shouldn't spread ourselves too thin. We give you 200 words and phrases because we want to satisfy your thirst—not drown you!

There is another consideration as well. My mother tongue is English and I have read many books on English words and sayings. And you know what? A large portion I have never heard in my lifetime! Never! Some Spanish language phrasebooks are just as all-inclusive. But how do you know if that phrase was known and used by 100 people or a 100,000? We save you the time by sorting that out for you. We hand you an eclectic selection to practice and perfect.

How to use this book

Guatemalan Spanish: Speak like a Native! is divided into ten sections. Check out the table of contents and jump to the one that most interests you. Others read just one entry a day and then try to practice that new word or phrase as soon as possible. That way you *own* it.

Only one or two terms appear on each page. This will help your focus. For many entries a literal meaning is provided. This often sounds unnatural in English, but can be an aid to memory. Where the headings **"In a nutshell"** appear, we help you understand the origin behind many of the popular sayings that make Guatemalan Spanish such a delight to listen to. Sometimes we throw in a tip or two as to when using that phrase would be appropriate. Just a few pronunciations are provided for words that may initially throw foreigners for a loop.

In the main text, Guatemalan words and phrases appear in **bold type.** Shortly thereafter the translation of the phrase will appear in *italics*. In many cases, sample sentences were ripped right from the headlines or newspaper articles that have appeared in the Guatemalan press. *GringoGuide200* merely collects these quotes and they do not represent the opinion of the author. Since Spanish and English differ in punctuation styles, we here favor the English style even in Spanish quotes.

Lastly, feel free to use the terms listed here in everyday speech. Our selection is informal, but devoid of vulgarities.

Having understood this, **¡Aprovéchete Matías, que esto no es de todos los días!** (See page 82.) Dive in and enjoy!

1

A CONVERSATION PIECE

¡A la gran!

Literal meaning: To the great!

In a nutshell: This means: *"Wow!"* It is actually a euphemism, because the complete phrase makes reference to a certain lady of the night. Even so, the original idea has now been mostly forgotten, and this has become the exclamation that will most naturally occur to a Guatemalan.

"¿Sabés qué? ¡Estoy encinta!"
"¡A la gran!"
Translation: "Guess what? I'm pregnant!"
"You're kidding!"
Many times the phrase is shortened to: **"¡A la!"**
Another less common variation is: **"¡Ulu grun!"**

¡Aguas!

Literal meaning: Waters!

In a nutshell: Years ago, before the advent of toilets, people would sometimes do their business in a bucket. Imagine someone throwing the nasty contents out of a two-story window! To protect those below, they would first shout out: **"¡Aguas!"** For that reason, the term means: *"Watch out!"*

CAUTION: HARD TORTILLAS!

If you venture into the more seedy parts of town, your host might warn you: "Tené mucho cuidado por allí. **Te pueden puyar con tortilla tiesa."** This is complete hyperbole, because it literally means: "Be careful over there. *They can stab you even with hard tortillas."* This exaggerated speech suggests that the area is so bad that even the common tortilla could be used as a deadly weapon.

¡Chish!

In a nutshell: *Interjection of disgust.* When a politician had the audacity to ask a poor street vendor for a discount on a very small item, the seller retorted:
"¡Chish! ¡Usted gana más que yo!"
Translation: *"You disgust me!* You make more money than I do!"
This is the perfect thing to say to a child who is about to stick something filthy in his mouth.

¡Qué buena onda!

Literal meaning: What a good wave!

In a nutshell: This common informal expression equates to *"How wonderful!"* or *"Great!"*
"¡Me ofrecieron una beca!"
"¡Qué buena onda!"
Translation: "They offered me a scholarship!"
"That's awesome!"

¡Qué de a sombrero!

Literal meaning: How hat-like!

In a nutshell: When a person is upset, he may throw his hat down in disgust. So this is the protest when someone is trying to take advantage of a situation.

When some public bus drivers suggested that government subsidies be eliminated and passengers use prepaid cards instead of cash, one reader responded: "Me he dado cuenta que hay una buena cantidad de los buses parados, ya sea que estén tirados en talleres o simplemente, como no son horas pico de pasaje, los sacan de su ruta y así quieren el subsidio cabalito, **¡qué de a sombrero!"**

Translation: "I am aware that a good number of the buses aren't running. Or during lower-revenue, non-peak hours they take them off the route. Even so, they want their complete subsidy! *What nerve!*"

¡Ydiay!

(pronounced ee-dee-EYE)

Literal meaning: And from there!

In a nutshell: When I first heard this exclamation, it sounded like a grunt to me. But it is one of the most common ways to complain or protest any action. For example, you purchase something and the cashier tries to shortchange you. You could say:

"¡Ydiay! ¿Y el resto?"

Translation: *"Hey! What's the deal?*
Where's the rest?"

¿Qué onda vos?

Literal meaning: What is your wave?

In a nutshell: When we see a good friend in the street, it would be far too dry to merely use a standard **"¿Cómo estás?"** Instead, use this Guatemalan favorite, which comes across more like: *"Hey, what's up?"*

¿Querés un tu café?

Literal meaning: Do you want a your coffee? [sic]

In a nutshell: This is a grammar teacher's worst nightmare, because the syntax, or word order, of this sentence is completely wrong. Normally, a person would only ask: Do you want a coffee? The personal pronoun **tu** (your) is out of place. Why? According to some estimates, as much as sixty percent of the country speaks an indigenous language. This kind of sentence came about by talking local languages and merely substituting the translation word for word. But no worries! Play along with it! It will give your speech a ring of authenticity.

WATCH YOUR HEAD!

The odd grammatical structure above can lead to some humorous combinations. Suppose you want your friend to pass you a drinking glass. You would say: **"¿Querés un tu vaso?"** Of course, in Spanish this sounds exactly like: **"¿Querés un tubazo?"** This means: *"Do you want me to hit you over the head with a pipe?"* Ouch!

19

¿va'a?

Literal meaning: right?

In a nutshell: Guatemalans, just like the majority of their Central American neighbors, tend to cut off the final consonants in informal speech. This is especially true with the word for *true,* **verdad.** In this case, not only is the final *d* lopped off, the intermediate *erd* morphs into an *a*. The two *a*'s are only separated by a micropause, which is represented by an apostrophe. "Está bien chilero, **va'a?"** Translation: "It's really cool, *right?*" Listen carefully for this in everyday conversation, and repeat it again and again until it rolls off your tongue. You'll be well on your way to speaking bona fide Guatemalan Spanish!

barajearla más despacio

Literal meaning: Deal [the cards] more slowly

In a nutshell: There's nothing like a good card game. But in the heat of emotion your friend may deal out the cards so quickly that things get a little out of control. So if someone is explaining a matter so speedily that you can't really understand, just say: **"Barajeámela más despacio."** It's like saying: *"Give it to me nice and slow."*

bien

In a nutshell: Every Spanish student knows **bien** means *good*. But in Guatemala it also means *yes*. To make your speech more authentic, the next time someone asks you a yes or no question, respond with: **"Bien."**

"¿Te gustaría ir al cine esta noche?"
"Bien."
Translation: "Would you like to go to
the movies tonight?"
"Yes."

¡Brincos dieras!

Literal meaning: You should wish to jump!

To attain something seemingly impossible.
"Cuando yo sea grande, quiero ser neurocirujano."
"¡Brincos dieras!"
Translation: "When I grow up, I want to be a neurosurgeon."
"Well, don't hold your breath!"

cacho

Literal meaning: horn

A little bit.

"Sé un **cachito** de matemática."
Translation: "I know just *a little* about math."
It is also used to indicate approximate lengths of time.
"Ella tiene veinte años y un **cacho.**"
Translation: "She's twenty *something*."

chilero

Literal meaning: of or relating to chile, or peppers

In a nutshell: Guatemalans are not as given to hot, spicy foods as their Mexican neighbors. It is no surprise, then, that **chilero** usually has nothing to do with mouth-burning of any kind. Rather, here it takes on the meaning of *nice, good, or beautiful,* depending on the context.

"¡Qué **chilera** tu chumpa!"

Translation: "Boy, that's a really *beautiful* jacket!" (See **chumpa,** page 41.)

BLAZINGLY FAST

If you are familiar with the NBA's Miami Heat, you know that heat sometimes equals speed. So when someone does something **al chilazo,** it means *speedily.* "Me arreglaron la burra **al chilazo.**" Translation: "They fixed the bus *super quick."* (See also **burra,** page 107.)

chinto

A strong color. "Trajo una blusa amarilla, pero era de un amarillo **chinto.**" Translation: "She brought a yellow blouse, but it was a *neon yellow.*"

chipuste

In a nutshell: This refers to *gobs* of something, usually with a connotation of frustration. "Dejé que mi sobrinito pintara la casa, y el patojo dejó **chipustes** de pintura por todo el piso." Translation: "I let my nephew paint the house, and the kid left *disgusting gobs* of paint all over the floor."

de plano

Literal meaning: flatly

In a nutshell: Since **plano** in Spanish means *flat,* when you first hear this, it may seem out of place. This is a local idiom, which means *completely,* or *totally.*
"Ese patojo **de plano** está loco."
Translation: "That guy's *completely* nuts."

Es pan para mi matate.

Literal meaning: It is bread for my bag.

In a nutshell: A **matate** is a mesh bag used by farmers and others to gather fruits and vegetables during the harvest. On other occasions it was used to carry the daily bread home. Just as the **matate** contains valuable food, our mind carries our thoughts. This expression has come to mean *food for thought* or *lessons for life* and often appears as a headline for editorials.

dos que tres

Literal meaning: two or three

In a nutshell: Don't be surprised if one day you ask a local how he's doing and his response is: **"Dos que tres."** Immediately you will mentally reach for your calculator and wonder what's up with the numbers. But there is no math involved in this one. It merely means *"so, so."* This construction also came from Mayan languages such as Cachiquel, Kekchi, and Quiche. In these languages **dos que tres** means *some*.

"¿Cómo está tu abuelito?
"Dos que tres."
Translation: "How's your grandpa doing?"
"He's *getting by.*"

Fíjese que...

Literal meaning: Look...

In a nutshell: Ask someone an incriminating question and watch him squirm. Similarly, when a Guatemalan gets uncomfortable or feels that he must offer an excuse of some kind, the sentence invariably begins with this. **"Fíjese,** profesora, que iba a hacer la tarea, pero anoche, **fíjese** que se nos murió el mish y en toda la bulla se me olvidó." Translation: *"Well, ummm,* teacher, I was going to do the homework, but *you now what?* Our cat died last night and in all the ruckus, I forgot."

IF YOU CAN'T REMEMBER, GO EAST!

When we as English speakers are at a loss for words, we begin to insert mannerisms like *and, uh, umm,* and so forth. The Spanish speaker, on the other hand, will invariably say **este**. When you say **este**, hold out the final e about two or three times as long as the first vowel. The longer you hold it, the more obvious it will be that you are groping for words. So just head east, young man!

hasta donde el Diablo dejó el caite

Literal meaning: to where
the Devil left his sandal

In a nutshell: Ever have to drive somewhere
so far and inaccessible that you thought you
would never get there? Though Guatemala
is relatively small, poor highways can make
the journey to certain towns quite arduous.
If someone later asks where you went, you
might reply: "Fui **hasta donde
el Diablo dejó el caite."**
Translation: "I went *all the way to Timbuktu.*"
Another option is **hasta donde Judas dejó
el caite,** that is, *where Judas
left his sandal.*

jalón

Literal meaning: the big pull

A ride. "Como ya no tengo carro, voy a pedir **jalón** para llegar al colegio." Translation: "Since I no longer have a car, I am going to ask for a *ride* to get to school."

len

A one-cent coin. "Lo siento, muchá, pero no tengo ni un **len.**" Translation: "I'm sorry, guys, but I don't even have a *penny.*"
The plural form **lenes** is used to mean *money in general.* "Aquí tenés tus **lenes.**" Translation: "Here's your *money.*"

muchá

Literal meaning: guys

In a nutshell: This form of address is likely a shortened form of **muchachos** and means *you guys,* but it encompasses much more than that. Implicit is a sense of camaraderie and of belonging. If you have the opportunity to work with a group of Guatemalans, just get their attention with **muchá,** and then voice your request.

"Muchá, ¿cuándo creen que terminaremos este proyecto?"
Translation: *"Hey guys,* when do you think we will finish this project?"

Patas, ¿para que te quiero?

Literal meaning: Feet, why do I need you?

In a nutshell: You will hear this childish phrase especially when someone has to leave in a hurry. "Cuando Juan vio a los pandilleros acercándose, dijo: **'Patas, ¿para que te quiero?'**" Translation: "When Juan saw the gang members approaching, he said: *'I need to make like a tree and leave!'*"

pelar

Literal meaning: to peel

In a nutshell: When we peel a fruit or vegetable, we chop away at its exterior. Those who criticize others do a similar figurative chopping. "Somos buenos para **pelar** antes de ver el cuadro completo." Translation: "We are good at *criticizing* before looking at the big picture."

pensando en los anteojos del gallo

Literal meaning: thinking about the rooster's sunglasses

In a nutshell: How many roosters have you seen wearing sunglasses? None, of course. This playful idiom means *being in deep thought, daydreaming*, or *being distracted.*

"En la tarde, iba manejando sobre la 19 calle de la zona 10, **pensando en los anteojos del gallo,** cuando un par de golpes secos sobre la ventanilla me regresaron al planeta tierra."

Translation: "In the afternoon I was driving on 19th Street in Zone 10, *completely in La La Land,* when two knocks on my windshield brought me back to Planet Earth."

pushito

In small increments. "Echále un **pushito** de sal a los frijoles." Translation: "Put a *pinch* of salt in the beans." Debts also may be paid off in this way. It sometimes occurs in the phrase **por pushitos,** *little by little.*

Sí, pues

Literal meaning: Yes, then

In a nutshell: You will find that Guatemalans rarely answer yes/no questions with a mere **sí.** Almost invariably, it comes out as **"sí, pues."** To make your speech more authentic, the next time you say **sí,** make sure to follow it with **pues.** For an even better response, see **"bien,"** page 21.

tanates

In a nutshell: Mexicans may blush at this term, which to them is a vulgarity. But, in Guatemala, it is extremely useful. **Mis tanates** means *my stuff,* or my things. Usually, it doesn't refer to items of great monetary value, but rather, stuff in general. Other great wildcard filler words include **bultos, cachibaches, chivas, chunches,** and **tiliches.** "Mi primo se fue con todo y sus **tanates.**" Translation: "My cousin left with all his *stuff.*"

Vengo en el carro de don Nando, ratos a pie y ratos andando.

Literal meaning: I came in Mr. Fernando's car, a while on foot and a while walking.

In a nutshell: Try this with your Guatemalan friends. If you happen to walk to visit someone, they may be surprised as to how you got there. When they ask, just offer this colorful saying. It's a humorous way to break the sad news that you had to come on foot and may get you an offer of the beverage of your choice.

vos

Literal meaning: you (familiar form)

If you learned Spanish in high school or college, in all likelihood you were never taught about **vos.** This is a local substitution for **tú,** but it has so much more personality! **Vos** is the pronoun for *you,* but it is only used among friends. You can definitely feel free to utilize it when talking to children.
To get your Guatemalan friends to talk to you this way, you might prod them with: **"Por favor, trátame de vos."** Translation: *"Please, use the pronoun* **vos** *when you talk to me."*
Vos is also used as a filler word at the end of sentences. "Fijáte, no he visto a tu primo **vos."** In this case, you probably wouldn't even translate it in English. "Hey, I haven't seen your cousin." Pay close attention to how locals use this special pronoun, and then practice it in everyday conversation. Soon, it will become second nature.

2

ALL IN THE FAMILY

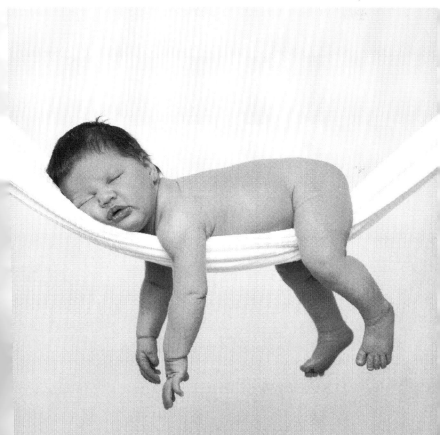

acuchuchar

In a nutshell: Everybody likes to be babied from time to time, and this is the verb for it in Guatemala. "Hay que **acuchuchar** a tu esposa ahora que está enfermita." Translation: "You've got to *pamper* your wife now that she's sick."

cashpiana

In a nutshell: *An illicit lover.* "Eso de falta de moral también es aplicable a la pareja del patriota donde el candidato anda exhibiéndose con su **cashpiana,** dejando en la banca a la esposa."
Translation: "The lack of morals also applies to the politician's marriage where the candidate struts around with his *mistress* and leaves his wife on the bench."
The masculine form is **cashpián.**

cercha

Literal meaning: a curved template,
or roof truss

In a nutshell: *A clothes hanger.* Try this: If you compliment someone on his or her clothing, follow up with: "Pero lo más bonito es la **cercha."** Translation: "Of course, what really makes it beautiful is the *hanger!*" Depending on to whom you say it, it could come across as a **piropo,** or *flirtatious comment.*

chamarra

In a nutshell: In Mexico a **chamarra** is a jacket, but in Guatemala it mostly refers to the *blankets* that keep you warm in bed. So if you are running late, offer this excuse: "Se me pegaron las **chamarras."** Translation: "I *got up late* today."

¡Chinchilete!

Literal meaning: [childish gibberish]

In a nutshell: Need to give away something, but not sure whom to give it to? Guatemalan children have this surefire method. Let's say a youngster wants to unload an extra mango. He would say: **"¿Chinchilete** este mango?"** And the first quick-minded kid who shouts back **"¡Yo machete!"** gets it. It's a childish raffle with no money involved.
Most likely a child in the English-speaking world would just say, *"Who wants this mango?"* And the first *"Me!"* gets it. In another version of this same practice **chinchilete** is substituted with **"Quién quilete."**

chivearse

Literal meaning: to be like a goat

In a nutshell: Goats are not exactly gregarious creatures. They are happiest aloof, left to themselves. Often when we are ashamed, we feel like doing the same. For that reason **chivearse** has come to mean *to become embarrassed.*
"Me alegró ver que mi traida no **se chiveó** cuando la presenté a la familia." Translation: "I was happy to see that my girlfriend didn't *get embarrassed* when I introduced her to the family."

chumpa

A jacket. "¿Dónde compraste esa **chumpa** de cuero vos?" Translation: "Where did you buy that leather *jacket?*"

cincho

(pronounced SEEN-choh)

In a nutshell: *Belt,* as the kind you wear around your waist. In many other Latin countries terms such as **cinto** or **faja** are used. A father may tell his child: "¡O me obedecés o te voy a dar un buen **cinchazo!"** Translation: "Either you listen, or you are going to get a good *whipping!*"

cincos

Literal meaning: fives

In a nutshell: Everyone knows **cinco** is *five* in Spanish. But when it is used as a plural noun, it refers to *marbles,* like the kind you played with as a kid. Speaking about available activities at a local fair, one report read: "Hay tiempo de trompos, de barriletes, y de **cincos."** Translation: "There will be time to play with tops, kites, and *marbles.*"

como hospiciano en feria

Literal meaning: like an orphan at the fair

In a nutshell: The poor orphans! Years ago they would get out only once or twice a year and would go to the Fair in Jocotenango. Imagine their jubilation! So when a friend is unusually jovial, just say: "Andás **como hospiciano en feria.**" Translation: *"You are as happy as a clam."*

cuaches

Twins. "Cuando nacieron los **cuaches,** los gastos de la familia se dispararon." Translation: "When the *twins* were born, our costs skyrocketed."

desguachipado

(pronounced days-watch-ee-PAH-doh)

Disheveled, messy dress and grooming. "Vestíte bien. No quiero que andes por las calles toda **desguachipada."** Translation: "Dress well. I don't want you walking through the streets *dressed like a bum*." (See also **pashtudo,** page 144.)

echarse un cuaje

Literal meaning: to throw a coagulation

In a nutshell: The verb **cuajar** means *to coagulate*, or *to solidify*. When we sleep, an observer may see that our body does something similar. We curl up as we find a comfortable position. So when a local **se echa un cuaje,** it means he is *taking a nap.*
"Voy a **echarme un cuaje,** mientras el bebé está durmiendo."
Translation: "I'm going *to take a nap* while the baby sleeps."

echar los perros

Literal meaning: to sick the dogs

In a nutshell: Every hunter values his hounds. Their acute sense of smell makes them ideal companions on the hunt. But when a Guatemalan sicks his dogs on someone, he is on a different sort of hunt: one of love.

This idiom means *to date*.

"Camilo le **está echando los perros** a María." Translation: "Camilo is *dating* María." Hopefully, Camilo isn't barking up the wrong tree! (See also **pitiar** and **cantinear,** page 51.)

Está colgado como chorizo en tienda.

Literal meaning: He is hanging like a sausage in the store.

In a nutshell: Falling in love can have a powerful effect on a person, almost like a drug. So, in Guatemalan Spanish, a person in such a state is said to be **colgado como chorizo en tienda.** Sausages here are not usually hidden away in a cooler, but prominently on display in a store's entrance. The idea? Onlookers can tell what is going on without explanations.

"Ricardo, desde que conoció a Rut, **está colgado como chorizo en tienda."**

Translation: "Ricardo, ever since he met Rut, has been *head over heels in love."*

The same idea can be shortened to **está colgado.**

güiro

(pronounced WEE-roh)

Literal meaning: kid

In a nutshell: Boys will be boys! And this popular term for *boy* or *kid* captures the essence of the child at his mischievous best. In some contexts *rascal* captures the spirit better. One writer bemoaned: "En nuestra sociedad, en donde la subsistencia todavía es una triste prioridad, no es válido enviar a estudiar a los **güiros** por Q300 mensuales cuando a cambio pierden el tiempo y reciben una preparación que en nada les ayudará a subsistir."

Translation: "In our society, where just getting by is a sad priority, it is not worthwhile to send the *kids* to study for 300 quetzals a month when all they do is waste their time and receive an education that does nothing to help them get by."

ishto

Literal meaning: child

In a nutshell: Ishto means a *child* or *kid,* but it can have a somewhat negative connotation, by implying that he is in some way a nuisance. "¿Cómo se ponen a hacerle caso a un **ishto** mocoso que jamás ha trabajado en el estado?"
Translation: "How is it that suddenly you are starting to listen to a snot-nosed *brat* who never even worked for the government?"
As is seen in this example, it doesn't necessarily refer to a literal child. It could even mean here a *guy.* (See also **güiro,** page 47, and **patojo,** page 50.)

jaboneada

Literal meaning: soaping

In a nutshell: If as a child you ever let out an unexpected expletive at home, did your parents threaten to wash your mouth out with soap? If so, come clean! Sorry, all lathering aside, this clever Guatemalan metaphor is all about being scolded with words.

After a politician was lambasted in the media for his infantile campaign tactics, one person commented: "Ve pues, qué calmado comentó ahora don Edgar Juárez, como que le cayó bien la **jaboneada** de hace dos dias."

Translation: "Look at how calmly Edgar Juárez commented. It looks like the *tongue-lashing* he got two days ago did him some good."

llegarle a uno

Literal meaning: to get to someone

In a nutshell: Llegar is the verb *to arrive.* But in
this context, it takes on the sense of *liking* or *loving*
something or somebody. One man wrote in his blog:
"Soy chapín y Guate **me llega."**
Translation: "I'm Guatemalan and I *love* Guatemala."

patojo

In a nutshell: Hundreds of years ago when the
Spaniards arrived in Guatemala, the foreigners observed
native children running through the streets barefoot.
In Spanish sometimes a person's foot is humorously
called a **pata** (though usually reserved for animals).
So someone who walked about shoeless was called a
patojo. As time passed the term came to refer to any
child–with or without footwear. "Cuántos **patojos**
tiene?" Translation: "How many *children* do you have?"

50

pitiar

Literal meaning: to tie

In a nutshell: *To date or court.* **Pitas** are *cords,* and it's the local term for *shoestrings.* Of course, if a man is trying to win over the heart of a certain lady friend, he is trying to get a hold of the strings of her heart. So this is a fitting verb for *dating.*
"Juan le está **pitiando** a Elena, ¿va'a? Translation: "Juan is *going out with* Elena, right?"

RAISING THE BAR

Before you can date someone, you have to win over his or her heart. The verb for this locally is **cantinear,** which literally means *bar-hopping*. Apparently, some have found that special someone with visits down to the local canteen. "¿Supiste que Juan ya está **cantineándole** a María?" Translation: "Did you hear that Juan is *dating* María?"

quemar la canilla

Literal meaning: to burn the lower part of the leg

In a nutshell: Locally, the term **canilla** is used for the lower part of the leg. But if someone figuratively "burns your leg," it means they have *betrayed* you. It is often applied to marital infidelities.
"Marta le **quemó la canilla** a Juan."
Translation: "Marta *betrayed* Juan."
Another expression in the same vein is **quemar el rancho,** that is, *to burn the ranch down.*

Siempre hay un roto para un descosido.

Literal meaning: There is always a rip for every sewing that's come undone.

In a nutshell: In an article about two graffiti artists whose works were being put in public exposition, a reader wrote in: "Creo que esta es una de las tantas formas de expresión que la juventud ha adoptado, falta de cultura sería ignorarlo; **para cada roto hay un descosido."** Translation: "I think it's one of the many forms young people have adopted, and it would be a lack of culture to ignore it. *There's something for everyone."*

The saying also suggests that, romantically, *there's someone for everyone.* The abbreviated version is: **"Para un roto, un descosido."**

tapón

Literal meaning: the big drain plug

In a nutshell: Does your kitchen sink have a plug? When you stick it in the drain, a tight seal is formed. For that reason, a **tapón** is a *close, intimate friend,* someone who will stick with you through thick and thin. "Jorge siempre anda de **tapón** con Jacob." Translation: "Jorge and Jacob are *inseparable.*"

traida

(pronounced TRY-dah)

Literal meaning: the thing brought

Girlfriend. This archaic Spanish word never went out of style in Guatemala. "¿Y la **traida?** ¿No la trajiste? Translation: "And your *girlfriend?* Didn't you bring her?" The masculine version is **traido** for *boyfriend.* Another local word for girlfriend is **güiza,** sometimes spelled **wisa.** (See also **pitiar** y **cantinear,** page 51.)

3

A HARD
DAY'S WORK

achimero

A street vendor. "Cualquier **achimero** sabe que si invierte, va a ganar más dinero." Translation: "Any old *street vendor* knows that if he invests, he will earn more money." (See also **transero,** page 135.)

chambón

Literal meaning: a big job

In a nutshell: In Guatemalan Spanish a **chamba** is a *job,* especially one that is temporary. A **chambón,** on the other hand, is a *person who does poor quality work.* And a **chambonada** is a *botched job,* or *shoddy work.* "Esa carretera es una **chambonada.** Tiene poco tiempo y ya está lleno de baches." Translation: "That highway is nothing but a *botched job.* They just built it and it's already filled with potholes."

chaquetear

Literal meaning: to jacket

In a nutshell: This term celebrates the lobbyist in each of us. It used to be that when someone wanted to ingratiate himself with the person in charge, he would walk up to him and admire his **chaqueta,** or *suitcoat*, perhaps even caressing the lapels during conversation. The noun became a verb and locally means *to butter someone up*.

"No sé a quién **chaqueteó** Rolando para tener ese empleo en la Alcaldía. Translation: "I don't know who Rolando *kissed up to* in order to get that job at City Hall."

(See also **culebra,** page 60.)

¿Cómo te quedó el ojo?

Literal meaning: How did your eye end up?

In a nutshell: This is classic trash talk, Guatemalan style. Imagine the scene: You are in a tight soccer game. Finally, you break through the defense and score the game-winning goal! To top things off, you say, **"¿Cómo te quedó el ojo?"** to the goalie. It's like boasting in English: *"Look who's laughing now!"* Or perhaps: *"How do you like them apples?"* Or even: *"Stick that in your pipe and smoke it."*

cuchubal

In a nutshell: In rural Guatemala, where many subsist on a dollar a day, these small women's savings clubs—usually with a dozen or fewer members—play a key role in the local economy. Each person contributes a quota to a common fund and the sum is awarded monthly to a selected member.

"Otras fundaciones consideran la pobreza y las necesidades sociales un asunto de **cuchubal.**"
Translation: "Other foundations consider poverty and social needs a matter for the *local women's savings clubs.*"

culebra

Literal meaning: snake

In the Garden of Eden, it was the snake that approached Eve, pretending to be her friend—albeit with ulterior motives. In the same way today every school and every company has its brown-nosers and bootlickers. So if a Guatemalan calls someone a **culebra,** check the color of his nose! He is probably just buttering someone up to get his way.
"Manuel, ¡no seas **culebra!"**
Translation: "Manuel, don't be such a *brown-noser!*"
Another similar term is **arrastrado.**

cuque

In a nutshell: *A low-ranking military combatant.*
This everyday term for *soldier* has a slightly negative connotation. An article in one of the largest newspapers in the country pointed out: "Se sabe que son tres mil los **cuques** que apoyan a la Policía, a un costo de Q3 mil cada uno, más los gastos de movilización."
Translation: "It is known that some three thousand *soldiers* support the police, at a cost of three thousand quetzals each, plus deployment costs."
On the other hand, a high-ranking officer is called derogatively a **chafa** or **chafarote.**

SHODDY GOODS

Though **chafa** can denote a military leader, it is more often used to refer to *poor quality* goods. "Tus lentes son bien **chafas.**" Translation: "Your glasses are really *chintzy.*" Even poor Mickey Mouse is associated with cheap quality. "Esas liquadoras baratas son puro **miqui maus.**" Translation: "Those cheap blenders are nothing but *junk.*" Sorry, Mickey!

dar el piojo

Literal meaning: to give the louse

In a nutshell: Imagine this: your friend is crushed because he just found out he has lice. And the worst thing of all is that he got it from you! How would you feel? Like a total loser! This unsavory metaphor means *to fail* or *to give up.* One opinion writer lamented how the government constantly tricks the public into raising taxes.

"Por ello es que siempre **damos el piojo** y los políticos se salen con la suya."
Translation: "That's why we always *throw in the towel* and the politicians get what they want."

El buey solo se lame.

Literal meaning: The ox licks himself without any help.

In a nutshell: The ox is known for its power and to this day in Guatemala can be seen pulling heavy loads. But if it gets a little scraped up, does it really need someone to come and lick its wounds? Of course not! So the idea behind this saying is: *We can take care of our own.*

When political tensions arose recently between Venezuela and Paraguay, the following comment was posted in a local paper: "A los únicos que Paraguay le debe explicaciones es a su propio pueblo, lo que digan o piensen los demás que no les quite el sueño, **¡el buey sólo bien se lame!"** Translation: "The only ones Paraguay has to answer to are her own people. They shouldn't lose sleep over what others say or think. *They are big boys now.*"

Entra como gerente y sale como albañil.

Literal meaning: He comes like the manager and leaves like the bricklayer.

In a nutshell: When does the boss show up? Whenever he pleases. And when does the bricklayer go home? Punctually when his shift ends. This playful saying is used in reference to the worker who comes and goes as he pleases, with little regard for the clock.

hacer la campaña

Literal meaning: to do the campaign

In a nutshell: Getting elected takes a lot of work. No one could do it without help. So this clever phrase means *to do a favor*. "¿No podés ir a la tienda para comprarme un mango? ¡Porfa, **hacéme la campaña!"** Translation: "Could you please go to the store and buy me a mango? Please! *Do me a favor!*"

hacerse bolas

Literal meaning: to become balls

To get tangled up, mixed up, or *confused.*
"En la entrevista para un nuevo empleo
cuando comenzaron a hacerme preguntas,
me hice bolas."
Translation: "On the job interview when they
began asking questions, *I got all flustered.*"

FOUL BALL

When a ball is rolling, the open floor offers little resistance. It's appropriate, then, that **bolas** in certain contexts can mean *rumors.* **"Andan las bolas** que van a vender aquí." Translation: *"Rumor has it* that they are going to sell this place." The same idea is contained in the expression **"Se regó la bola."** This means *the word's out,* and the matter is public knowledge.

hacerse un queso

Literal meaning: to make oneself a cheese

In a nutshell: Making cheese isn't easy. And making yourself into a cheese can be far more difficult! So if someone says, **"Me hice un queso,"** it means he went out of his way to please.

One writer complained that the service at one hotel was so bad he had to get up and pick up the plates himself. He relates: "Cuando el [jefe de los meseros] cayó en la cuenta de su descuido, **se hizo un queso** para sacar el clavo."

Translation: "When the head waiter realized the lack of attention, he *bent over backwards* to make things right."

PROBLEMS, PROBLEMS...

Did you notice the use of the word **clavo** in the example above? Literally, a **clavo** is a *nail,* but here the writer is talking about a methaphoric nail: *a problem.* Due to a lack of honesty, one popular phrase goes like this: "Mientras no me cachen, no hay **clavo.**" Translation: "As long as I don't get caught, there's no *problem."*

kaibil

(pronounced KIGH-beel)

In a nutshell: A **kaibil** is a member of the special operations forces of the Guatemalan army, skilled in jungle warfare tactics and counter-insurgency operations.

"El testigo protegido no es **kaibil.**"
Translation: "The protected witness is not *a member of the Guatemalan special operations force.*"

Me agarraste de tu puerquito.

Literal meaning: You have taken me as your little piggie.

In a nutshell: Pity the poor pig! He is fattened, slaughtered, and taken to market, where every part of his body will be quartered and sold! So if someone says that you are taking him as his little piggie, back off! It means that he feels you are *taking advantage* of him.

"Cuando le pedí a Antonio que me hiciera un favor más, enojado me dijo: '¡Qué! **¿ya me agarraste de tu puerquito!'**"

Translation: "When I asked Antonio to do me one more favor, he responded angrily: 'What! *Am I your slave now?*'"

Another similar—but far less common— expression in the Eastern part of the country is **"Me agarraste de tu arce."**

merolicos

Literal meaning: food people

In a nutshell: Have you noticed that on many cable channels these days much programming is nothing more than paid infomercials, some of which last from 30 minutes to an hour? If you think that is a bit of overkill, meet the **merolicos,** who are the Guatemalan version of the walking, breathing infomercial. Usually, a **merolico** places himself in a public space with a microphone or megaphone and gives a lengthy sales speech to any passersby. Due to some of the dubious information sometimes involved, the word has, in some contexts, come to mean a *quack,* or *charlatan,* and is often applied to politicians.

"Pero, en general, podría decirse que la mayoría de comentarios que pululan en el ambiente no es más que charlatanería, peor que la usada por los **merolicos** en las plazas públicas."

Translation: "But, in general, it could be said that the majority of comments that are circulating out there are nothing more than charlatanry, worse than those used by the *street vendors* in the public plazas."

meterse en camisa de once varas

Literal meaning: to get into an eleven-**vara** shirt

In a nutshell: A **vara** is an old Spanish unit of measurement equal to about 33 inches. So an eleven-**vara** shirt would be more than 30 feet long! This obvious hyperbole means *to get into insurmountable difficulties.*
When an aged piano teacher decided to put on a recital for the first time in more than fifty years, he acknowledged: **"Me metí en camisa de once varas,** pero creo que ya recuperé mi técnica en un cincuenta por ciento, y espero que para el domingo esté mucho mejor."**
Translation: *"I'm really in over my head,* but I think I've got my technique back fifty percent, and I hope that by Sunday I'll be much better."

necesitar tecomates para nadar

Literal meaning: to need gourds to swim

In a nutshell: The **tecomate** is a kind of squash whose hard skin is used to make rustic spoons or drink glasses. If they are not perforated in any way, some people even use them as rudimentary flotation devices. For that reason, **necesitar tecomates para nadar** has come to mean *a crutch,* much in the way young children may use training wheels on their bicycles. After an opinion piece which suggested that there should be quotas to determine how many indigenous peoples and women should serve in public office, one man posted the following: "¿No será racismo asumir que un grupo **necesita tecomates para nadar?** Las mujeres y los indígenas son mayoría en el país, así que nadie les impide elegir a quienes prefieran." Translation: "Wouldn't it be racism to suggest that a group needs *a crutch?* Women and the indigenous are the majority in the country, and no one keeps them from electing whomever they may choose."

papa pelada

Literal meaning: peeled potato

In a nutshell: Ever peel a stack of potatoes? Your hands and back will be aching! That's why these days few are willing to do it. They prefer to have everything handed to them on a plate. In Guatemalan Spanish, they prefer to get their potatoes peeled. It's but a metaphor for *a life of ease.*

"Mucha gente quiere **la papa pelada** y que otro siembre para cosechar nosotros."

Translation: "Many people want *everything handed to them on a plate.* Let others sow so that we can reap."

pichirilo

An old, dilapidated car. "Eso me valió la odiosidad de varias condiscípulas sin ser baja ni morena ni llegar en [mi] **pichirilo."** Translation: "That earned me the scorn of several of my classmates without being short, dark-skinned and without arriving [at school] in *an old jalopy.*"

Pisto llama pisto.

Literal meaning: Money calls money.

In a nutshell: In Guatemala money is called **pisto.** And if you have some, it's easier to "call," or get, more. This is the equivalent of *the rich get richer.*
"El refrán popular de que **pisto llama pisto** no puede ser más cierto en el caso de la inversión mundial."
Translation: "The popular saying that *the rich get richer* couldn't be any more true than in the case of global investment."

A FOOL AND HIS MONEY...

Guatemala's currency is the **quetzal,** named after the national bird. But keep in mind that coins of any kind are called **fichas.** The one-cent coin is a **len;** the 25-cent piece, a **choca;** and 50 cents, a **tostón.** If someone tells you an item costs five **varas,** it means five *quetzals.* It's as informal as saying five *bucks,* but not worth nearly as much!

talacha

Literal meaning: chore

In a nutshell: The Girl Scouts sell cookies to raise funds. But in Guatemala, when university students desire to do the same, they organize a **talacha.** The difference is that on occasion the students have tried to obligate certain groups to buy their products. "Los estudiantes ya comenzaron la **talacha,** vendiendo calcomanías a pilotos de autobuses urbanos a un costo de Q25 cada uno." Translation: "The students started a *fund-raiser,* selling stickers to inner-city bus drivers at a cost of 25 quetzals each."

tener cuello

Literal meaning: to have neck

In a nutshell: Government red tape is enough to drive anyone crazy. In Guatemala, getting government permits can be especially time-consuming. And that's where your connections come in. Sometimes it's all about whom you know, or as Guatemalans would say, **tener cuello,** literally "having neck." This idiomatic expression means *to have pull* or *influence*.

"¿A quién vamos a mandar a la Alcaldía para sacar el permiso? Mejor mandemos a Enrique.
Es el único que **tiene cuello.**"
Translation: "Who are we going to send to City Hall to get the permit? Let's send Enrique. He's the only one *with pull*."

THE FIRST ONE IN THE ARK

Giraffes may be tall, slightly awkward animals, but don't sell them short. A Guatemalan joke asks: Which was the first animal in the ark? Answer: The giraffe. Why? "Es el único que **tenía cuello.**" Translation: "He's the only one *with pull*."

---

tener galleta

Literal meaning: to have a cracker

In a nutshell: Remember Popeye? When danger was near, he just scarfed down some spinach, and voilà! Instant strength! Apparently in Guatemala crackers will do the trick. **Tener galleta,** then, means *to be physically strong.*

"Agregó que a sus 72 años, se siente como de 15, y que 'todavía **tiene galleta** para gobernar.'"

Translation: "He added that even at 72 years of age, he feels like 15, and 'still has the *vim and vigor* to rule.'"

(See also **ñeque,** page 99.)

Todos se pasan la chibola.

Literal meaning: Everyone passes the marble.

In a nutshell: Whose fault is it? No one ever wants to take the blame. So we *pass the buck.* Locally, however, what gets passed is the figurative marble.
"Es penoso que los operadores de justicia no asuman una posición ética, y que unos a otros **se estén tirando la chibolita,** esquivando sus responsabilidades de administrar justicia."
Translation: "It is embarrassing that the operators of justice don't assume their ethical position. They just keep *passing the buck* amongst themselves, dodging their responsibilities to administer justice."

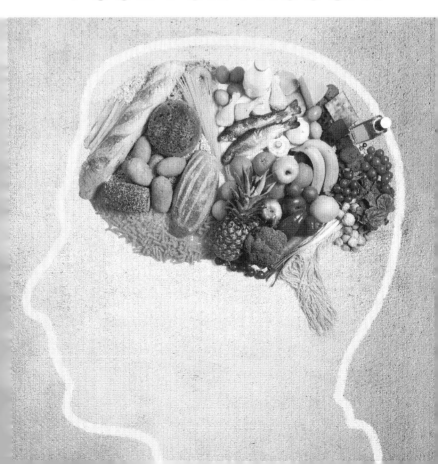

4

FOOD FOR THOUGHT

¡Échale más agua al caldo!

Literal meaning: Add more water to the soup!

In a nutshell: If guests come unexpectedly, rifle off this friendly saying. It is akin to: *"The more the merrier!"*

¡Ya son las doce, y la gallina no se coce!

Literal meaning: It's twelve o'clock and the hen still isn't cooked!

In a nutshell: Hungry? If so, when you arrive at your Guatemalan friend's house, just let out this hearty expression. It's like saying, *"Boy, am I starving!"* Surely your host will get the hint, and food will be on the way. Let's move on! This is making my mouth water.

alagartado

Literal meaning: lizard-like

In a nutshell: Ever watch lizards eat? They perch themselves motionless in a spot where they know creatures lower on the food chain will be passing by. Then, when a tasty specimen is in reach, their extremely long tongues rocket out and nab the unsuspecting victim. Due in no small part to their lightning-fast eating habits, if someone is said to be **alagartado,** it means he or she is a *voracious eater.* (See also **chucho,** page 109.)

champurrada

A type of local cookie. Try them with coffee or hot chocolate. Yummy!

¡Aprovéchate Matías, que esto no es de todos los días!

Literal meaning: Take advantage, Matthias, you don't get this every day.

In a nutshell: Ever notice that when you have guests over, sometimes they can be shy about eating because they don't want to appear greedy? If so, this phrase is a great icebreaker. Another option is just to say: **"¡Al ataque!"** Translation: *"Dig in!"*

chirmol

Literal meaning: A fresh salsa made from tomatoes, limes, onions, and cilantro.

In order to make that delicious **chirmol** for your tasty grilled meats, you throw all the ingredients in the blender and let it slice and dice. It turns into a delectable mixture. When we talk about others, often the facts get all blended together, and the result is another type of **chirmol:** *gossip.*
One headline read: **Chirmoles** chapines.
Translation: Guatemalan *gossip.*
Yet a third meaning is *a chaotic combination.*
One local called a large meeting of bishops "un verdadero **chirmol** religioso."
Translation: "a true religious *hodgepodge.*"
Another word for gossipy is **lengüetero.**

churrasco

Thinly-sliced beef flamed on the open grill—a Guatemalan delicacy. It is usually served with **chirmol** (see page 83) and guacamole. If you haven't had **churrasco,** you haven't been to Guatemala!

cuquitos

In a nutshell: These popsicles are *frozen fruit juices served in small plastic bags.*
"Vendía helados y **cuquitos** en las tiendas de su pueblo, pero lo que ganaba apenas alcanzaba para que él y su familia pudieran comer."
Translation: "He sold ice cream and *popsicles* in his town, but he barely earned enough for him and his family to eat."

fiambre

In a nutshell: A local *chef's salad,* prepared with upwards of 50 ingredients, which is served on All Saint's Day and The Day of the Dead. Why? Guatemalans used to take the dish to the cemetery as a way of appeasing their deceased relatives. Figuratively, it has come to mean an *unusual mixture.* "Nuestro gobierno es un **fiambre** de varios estilos y no se puede tipificar de manera precisa." Translation: "Our government is a *mixture* of many styles that cannot be accurately categorized."

mosh

Oatmeal, usually slow cooked for more than an hour until it becomes a thick drink. In this form it can be called an **atol.** It is also used figuratively to mean *strength.* "Hay que decir que se le debe meter mucho **mosh** a la prevención, la denuncia y participación ciudadana." Translation: "It must be said that a lot of *effort* has to be put into prevention and correct reporting of crime as well as citizen involvement."

hacerse de la boca chiquita

Literal meaning: to make like
you have a small mouth

In a nutshell: At mealtime no one wants to
be perceived as a glutton. That's why more
than a few need to be coaxed into eating. So
you might say to such a person: **"¿Por qué
te hacés de la boca chiquita?"**
This idea is also used figuratively, as shown
in the following example: "Los dirigentes del
gobierno anterior no pueden **hacerse de la
boca chiquita,** pues ellos también echaron
mano del recurso, si bien lo utilizaron
quizá más selectivamente."
Translation: "The former government leaders
can't *feign their innocence,* since they too
stuck their hands in the cookie jar, though
perhaps doing it more selectively."

pajilla

Straw, as in the drinking variety. "Katia,
¿no querés una **pajilla** para tu agua?"
Translation: "Katia, don't you want a *straw*
for your soft drink?"

A WATERED-DOWN DRINK?

When you are invited out to eat, sooner or later someone will ask you if you want **agua.** To the English speaker, the first idea that comes to mind is *water.* But in Guatemala **agua** also means a *soft drink.* If you would like literal water, ask for **agua pura.** What comes in the pipes from the street is **agua entubada,** and it is not always potable, depending on where you live.

poporopo
(pronounced poh-poh-ROH-poh)

In a nutshell: *Popcorn.* The generic term for this in Latin America is **palomitas de maíz.** But the Guatemalan term is far more colorful. Very likely it is an example of onomatopoeia, that is, a word that mimics the sounds associated with the word itself.
"Hijo, si te portás bien, te compro unos **poporopos** esta noche en el cine."
"Son, if you behave, I'll buy you some *popcorn* tonight at the movies."
Caramelized and rolled into a ball, it's called **alboroto.**

poyo

There's no chicken in this **poyo!** With this spelling, it refers instead to a *wood-burning stove.* "En la comunidad de San José Cabén, en San Pedro Sacatepéquez, el uso de telar es tan común como el del **poyo** para cocinar." Translation: "In the community of San José Cabén, en San Pedro Sacatepéquez, the use of the loom is as common as the *wood-burning stove* for cooking." Want to try one out? Don't be chicken!

shuquío

(pronounced shew-KEY-oh)

A bad smell. "¡Guácala! Esos frijoles ya tienen **shuquío."** Translation: "Gross! Those beans *smell terrible!*"

Salió más caro el caldo que los frijoles.

Literal meaning: The broth was more expensive than the beans.

In a nutshell: Ever heard of a Pyrrhic victory? It is a triumph that costs so many lives and resources that, in the end, it's not worth the steep price. When some officials began throwing around the idea of trying to incriminate those who participated in the guerrilla warfare of the 1980s, one opinion columnist responded: "Conocer la verdad no tiene nada de malo. Pero, por donde nos están llevando, **'el caldo nos saldrá más caro que los frijoles.'"** Translation: "There's nothing wrong with knowing the truth. But with the direction they are leading us, we are headed for *a hollow victory.*"

shuco

In a nutshell: *A locally made hot dog with all the fixings.* Typically, a **shuco** comes with cooked cabbage and topped with your choice of guacamole, ketchup, mustard and mayonnaise. In Guatemala City try out the **shucos** from the streets around the famous Liceo Guatemala School. There's even a local chain called "Los Shuquitos," which prepares these funky franks.

YOU DIRTY DOG

Shuco can also mean *dirty.* "Mira ¡qué **shucos** tus zapatos!" Translation: "Look how *filthy* your shoes are!" In another context, it can mean *rotten.* "No te comas esa naranja, ya está **shuca.**" "Don't eat that orange, it's *rotten.*" In reality, the meaning of *dirty* came before the hot dog. Since these are usually sold in the streets, people know they are not the most hygienically prepared foods. But they eat them anyway, because taste trumps cleanliness.

Son como los de Cobán, que solo comen y se van.

Literal meaning: They are like those from Cobán, who only eat and leave.

In a nutshell: Ever have to apologize for having to eat and run? If so, you'll love this Guatemalan alternative. Just say: "Lo siento. Hoy **soy como los de Cobán, que solo comen y se van."** Translation: *"I'm sorry to just eat and run."*

súchiles

In a nutshell: *A fermented drink made from corn, barley, ginger, and pineapple rinds.* It is not a taste for the faint of heart. In fact, one blogger described it this way: "It tastes like all the ingredients got together, made a suicide pack, leaped in a jar of water, drowned, and their bloated remains strained out days later, and the liquid is served." (See also **shuquío,** page 89.)

tilinte

Stretched out. If someone has really pigged out, it could be said of him: "Quedó bien **tilinte.**" Translation: "He's *stuffed to the gills.*"

utz pin pin

Delicious. **Utz** means *good* in many of the Mayan languages. "Estos frijoles están **utz pin pin.**" Translation: "These beans are *delicious.*"

READY TO BURST

The next time you've eaten to your heart's content and can't manage another bite, just say this: **"Tilinte estoy."** This literally means, "I'm stretched tight." The basic meaning is: *"I'm stuffed."*

Un chucho menos, un pan más.

Literal meaning: One less dog, one more bread.

In a nutshell: Here's a great line for your next dinner party. If you invite a large group and someone at the last minute calls informing he can't make it, just make an informal announcement. "Muchá, Rodrigo dice que no puede venir. . . así que **un chucho menos, un pan más."** Translation: "Rodrigo's not coming. . . *so there's more for us!*" (See also **chucho,** page 109.)

yuca

Literal meaning: cassava

In a nutshell: Ever tried to cook raw cassava? Although likened to a potato, it is tougher and more resistant. Even cooked, it still doesn't get down to a potato's texture. For this reason, if someone is said to be **yuca,** it means he or she is *difficult, complicated* or *strict.* "Mi profesor de matemática es bien **yuca."** Translation: "My math teacher is really *strict.*"

5

THE BODY HUMAN

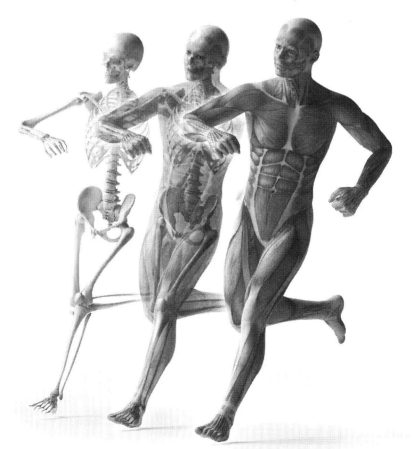

A ése no le gana una olla de tamales.

Literal meaning: A pot full of tamales can't keep up with that guy.

In a nutshell: Imagine the scene. Grandma is making tamales in an enormous pot on an open fire and puts a lid on top to bring it all to a boil. Of course, when the pressure builds, the lid will stammer and snort puffs of hot steam. And the decibel level will rise to a clamor. What a fitting metaphor for the insufferable snorer! So when you walk by grandpa's room and the curtains are nearly being sucked off the wall, it's the right time to let this popular saying roll off your lips.

chenco

Literal meaning: wobbly

In a nutshell: People who are crippled can be described as **chenco.** And so can wobbly tables. "Después de que operaran a mi abuelito, ha quedado un poco **chenco."** Translation: "After they operated on my grandpa, he's been a little *gimpy.*"

chilaca

In a nutshell: Informal term for *armpit.* "Andá, comprá un desodorante. Te apesta la **chilaca."** Translation: "Go get yourself some deodorant. Your *armpit* stinks!"

colgar los tenis

Literal meaning: to hang up
your tennis shoes

In a nutshell: When an athlete hangs up his tennis shoes, he is probably retiring from the sport. But this popular phrase speaks of a much more permanent retirement. It is a euphemism for *death*. "Panchito ya **colgó los tenis.**" Translation: "Panchito *kicked the bucket*." (See also **petatear,** page 145.)

hacer bish

In a nutshell: *To urinate.* This varies from the standard Spanish **orinar.** "Voy a ir a **hacer bish.**" Translation: "I am going *to pee*."

con pie y jeta

Literal meaning: with foot and mouth

In a nutshell: *Completely.* This disdainful phrase emphasizes the totality with which an accused should be brought to justice. It is similar to saying *lock, stock, and barrel* in English, but with a decidedly negative connotation. When a group of government officials were accused of perpetrating a multi-million-dollar heist just outside the international airport, one disgusted man posted the following: "Si es como dicen, hay que traerlos **con pie y jeta** de regreso." Translation: "If it's as they say, you better *get their butts* back here."

ñeque

Literal meaning: strength

In a nutshell: "¡Qué **ñeque!** " Translation: "Man, are you *strong!*" (See also **"ONE STRONG CAT,"** page 117, and **talishte,** page 165.)

nalgón

Literal meaning: big butt

In a nutshell: The most prominent body part of a coward is his hind end, because that's all his enemies see when he takes off running! "¡No seas **nalgón!**" Translation: "Don't be a *scaredy cat!*"

sholco

In a nutshell: This term came from a Mayan expression that meant "between two separated things." Nowadays it means *missing teeth*.
"El viejo está **sholco.**" Translation: "The old man is *missing some teeth*."

shola

In a nutshell: Forget about the generic Spanish **cabeza.** Locally, this is the wonderful alternative for *head,* and can be used in many contexts. "Dan ganas de meter la **shola** en la tierra como el avestruz." Translation: "You feel like sticking your *head* in the dirt like an ostrich." When four airport security agents were arrested for money laundering, one reader wrote: "No les va a alcanzar el pisto que les dieron (10,000 por **shola**) para pagar la [mordida] en la cárcel." Translation: "The money they were given (10,000 per *head)* isn't going to be enough for them to even pay the bribe in jail."

Quebrarse la shola means *to rack your brain.* On the other hand, if someone says, "No me da la **shola,"** it means: "I can't wrap *my brain* around it," or "I'm just *not smart enough* for this."

HAVING YOUR HEAD ON STRAIGHT

If your **shola** is working properly, people may describe you as **sheka,** or *intelligent.* One classified ad read: "Se busca ingeniero en electrónica/estudiante **sheka.**" Translation: "Electronic engineer/*bright* student needed."

101

patatush

In a nutshell: What happens when you hear tragic news? If you know the victim, your blood pressure may suddenly drop, causing you to faint. That phenomenon is encompassed by the term **patatush.** Rarely is it used literally, but rather, as an exaggeration for effect. "Cuando María escuchó que su hija se hizo un tatuaje en la cara, casi se le da un **patatush.**" Translation: "When María heard that her daughter got a tattoo on her face, she *nearly fainted.*" A synonym is **shucaque,** which can be used in like circumstances.

timba

In a nutshell: In standard Spanish, this is **barriga.** "Porque hasta el pobre y necesitado reconoce que no es el pan de hoy lo que llena la **timba,** sino la libertad de producir y crecer lo que colma el pecho de orgullo." Translation: "Because even the poor and needy know that it is not today's bread that fills the *belly.* It's the freedom to create and grow that fills our chests with pride." If you are called **timbón,** you have a *big belly.*

6

ANIMAL KINGDOM

A cada coche le llega su sábado.

Literal meaning: For each pig his Saturday eventually comes.

In a nutshell: In the past, it seems that Saturday was when a fattened pig would be taken to the slaughterhouse. For the poor pig, Saturday meant death. So today when someone gets his "just desserts" for misconduct, this saying enters into play. When two policemen ran off the road and pinned a married couple against a wall, injuring them, one blogger wrote: "La gente no habrá querido denunciarlos por miedo a venganzas ...pero **a cada coche se le llega su sábado.** Ahora les tocó a estos imbéciles." Translation: "People would not have wanted to report them for fear of retaliation. But *everyone will have his day of reckoning.* Now for these idiots their time has come." By the way, policemen are known collectively as **la chonta.**

A veces el pato nada, y a veces ni agua toma.

Literal meaning: Sometimes the duck swims, and sometimes it doesn't even drink water.

In a nutshell: Ducks love water and spend most of their time in it. But when times are tough, sometimes there's not even enough to drink. This, then, is the equivalent of *feast or famine.* Sometimes in life you get the bear, and other times, the bear gets you!

DON'T CRASH YOUR PIG!

In several Latin American countries, including Spain and Mexico, **coche** is the word for a *car*. When Guatemalans speak with other Latins, this can lead to confusion. If someone says: "Choqué con un **coche** que se me metió," it could mean either "I crashed into a *pig* that got in my way" or "I crashed into a *car* that got in my way." So, don't be a pig! If you are talking about cars, use the term **carro.** On the other hand, since **coche** means *pig*, if someone is described as being **coche** or **cochino,** it means they are *dirty* or *filthy.*

buitrear

Literal meaning: to vulture

In a nutshell: Vultures are probably not one of your favorite animals. Known for regularly regurgitating, they are true scavengers. It's fitting, then, that Guatemalans turned their name into a verb, which means *to vomit.* "¡Uff! ¡Qué ganas de **buitrear!**" Translation: "Yuck. I could *puke!*" Another form is **echar el buitre.**

chivo

Literal meaning: goat

In a nutshell: Do you remember those really hard history exams in high school? There was always at least someone in class who wrote out the answers on a tiny sheet of paper and folded it down to the size of a pin. Then, when the teacher wasn't around, he would quickly pull out his *cheat sheet* and scribble down some of the harder answers. In Guatemala, that sheet is called a **chivo.** Just remember: if you get caught, you will really get your teacher's goat!

burra

Literal meaning: female donkey

In a nutshell: Donkeys have been known to carry their load and then some. It is no surprise, then, that the natives have coined this colorful metaphor to describe the local buses. "¡Apuráte o te va a dejar la **burra!"**
Translation: "Hurry up or you are going to miss the *bus!*" A bus can also be called a **camioneta** and sometimes, just like in English, a **bus.**

BRUSH UP!

The bus driver, of course, is called the **chofer.** But, curiously enough, the fellow who takes your money is called a **brocha,** which literally means *a brush,* like those for painting. Apparently, he brushes your money right out of your pockets!

chompipe de la fiesta

Literal meaning: turkey of the party

In a nutshell: In standard Spanish, turkey is **pavo.** But locally it's a **chompipe.** It is one of holiday season's traditional foods. Of course, when those parties are coming around, pity the poor turkey! His days are numbered! For that reason, the **chompipe de la fiesta** is the *scapegoat,* the one that always gets blamed for the latest crisis. One writer penned: "Quienes pagan **el chompipe de la fiesta** son los menos privilegiados y, obviamente, las personas con mayores probabilidades de ver menoscabada su calidad de vida." Translation: "The *ones who pay the broken plates* are the underprivileged and, obviously, the persons with the greatest chances of seeing their quality of life diminished." In some parts of the country, the gobbler is also known as a **chunto.**

THE TURKEY TRAVELER

Since turkeys meander around quite a bit, Guatemalans have turned the word for this animal into a verb: **chompipear.** It means *to aimlessly wander.*

chucho

Literal meaning: dog

In a nutshell: Have you ever been around when Fido gets his bone? Would you dare reach out and try to snatch his food away? Not if you value your fingers! That highlights our canine friend's voracity. So if someone is called a **chucho,** it means he is a *glutton,* a quality that English speakers would equate more with a pig. If in a soccer game (see **chamusca,** page 121) a player is called a **chucho,** he is a *ball hog.* On the other hand, a **cola de chucho,** or *dog's tail,* is *someone who is always out and about.*

THE LITTLE DOGGIES YOU EAT!

One traditional food is **chuchitos de loroco.** If a **chucho** is a dog, then **chuchitos** should mean *little dogs.* But don't worry, dog lovers! **Chuchitos** actually are just *small tamales.* And **loroco** refers to the *edible flowers of the Fernaldia pandurata vine,* often added for extra flavor and even used as a topping on pizza! Hot dog!

109

Chucho no come chucho.

Literal meaning: Dogs don't eat dogs.

In a nutshell: Dogs don't eat other dogs. Everyone knows that. The idea here is that people who are from the same organization, or who are on the same level economically or otherwise, should not try to dominate one another. Thieves, for example, don't generally steal from other thieves.

Following an article about possible genocide charges that were being brought against former government leaders, one reader added: "No esperemos una sentencia condenatoria, **chucho no come chucho."** Translation: "Let's not expect a guilty verdict, because *the higher ups take care of their own.*"

como pizote

Literal meaning: like a coati

In a nutshell: The coati, locally known as the **pizote,** is an animal found in the forests throughout Central America. The male is known for always walking alone. "Ramón, siempre te veo andando **como pizote** en las calles." Translation: "Ramón, I always see you walking *all by yourself*."

de malas pulgas

Literal meaning: of bad fleas

In a nutshell: Ever see a dog with a bad case of fleas? The poor beast is miserable. And when people are similarly unhappy, it puts them in a *bad mood.* That's the idea behind this common canine comparison. "Cuando llamé al servicio al cliente, me salió una operadora **de malas pulgas.**" Translation: "When I called customer service, I got an operator who *woke up on the wrong side of the bed*."

El que es perico, dondequiera es verde.

Literal meaning: He who is a parakeet is green everywhere.

In a nutshell: Pericos, or *parakeets,* are green. Their greenness isn't altered in any way by their constantly changing geographic location. So when a person moves or starts working a new job, this saying comes into play. It means that if you are good, you will be good wherever you go. Keep in mind that it is not used to compliment others; rather, it smacks of braggadocio.

"Cuando Enrique iba a comenzar su nueva posición de vicepresidente, a sus compañeros jactó: **"El que es perico, dondequiera es verde."** Translation: "When Enrique was going to begin his new position as vice president, he bragged to his workmates: *"When you're good, you're good."*"

gastar pólvora en zanates

Literal meaning: to waste gunpowder
on black birds

In a nutshell: Seen throughout Central America,
zanates are fairly large birds with iridescent,
black plumage. They can sometimes be a
nuisance. But would it be worth it to shoo them
off with guns? Save your gunpowder! The idea
behind this popular idiom is that we shouldn't
waste our time on minor issues.
There are bigger fish to fry.

hacer de chivo los tamales

Literal meaning: to make the tamales
out of goat meat

In a nutshell: Tamales are one of the delicacies of
Guatemalan cuisine. But usually they are made with
pork or chicken and other ingredients. If someone
were to slip in a little goat meat, then they are trying
to cheat or *swindle* you. When the government
raised taxes once again, an opinion writer lamented:
"Si usted encuentra que un empleado o dependiente
suyo le está **haciendo de chivo los tamales,**
¿qué hace? ¿Le aumenta el sueldo? ¿Lo premia?"
Translation: "If you find that one of your employees
is *fleecing* you, what do you do? Increase his pay?
Reward him?"

mano de mono

Literal meaning: the monkey hand

In a nutshell: Would you think of leaving your valuables with a monkey? What chance is there that such a primate would respect your property? None whatsoever. For that reason, if someone is said to be doing a **mano de mono,** it means he is *stealing.* "En la mayor parte de obras que se ejecutan siempre hay **mano de mono** y cheques debajo de la mesa para taparle la boca a los dizque observadores." Translation: "In the majority of [public] works that are carried out there are always *sticky fingers* and checks given under the table to shut the mouths of the so-called observers."

más perdido que chucho en procesión

Literal meaning: more lost than a dog in a procession

In a nutshell: Whether for a funeral or some religious festival, processions are common in Guatemala. And, invariably, mingled amongst the marching hordes there is a happy dog or two. Of course, these canine party crashers have no idea what the celebration is all about. They're just along for the excitement. For that reason, **andar como chucho en procesión** means *to be completely lost, following the crowd without any rhyme or reason.*
"Estos pobres diputados están **más perdidos que chucho en procesión.**" Translation: "These poor congressmen *have no idea what they are doing and are just along for the ride.*"

mish

In a nutshell: In the Mayan languages **mix** is the word for *cat*. Since the *x* is given an *sh* sound in Mayan, the spelling has been adjusted for Spanish. So don't call your **gato!** That would be a big **mish**take! Use the local word!

On the other hand, if someone is described as **amishado,** it means he is *timid,* or *shy,* characteristic of our feline friends. "Elena es tan **amishada** que le cuesta hacer nuevos amigos." Translation: "Elena is so *bashful* that she has a hard time making new friends."

ONE STRONG CAT

How strong are you? Let's see. Make a muscle. That bulge in your arm, however puny, in Guatemala is said to be a **gato.** In contrast, when Mexicans make a muscle, it conjures up a **conejo,** or *bunny.* In either case, keep pumping that iron until your "cats" morph into a roar! "Ahora que vas al gimnasio, ¡qué clase de **gatos** tenés! Translation: "Now that you are going to the gym, man you've got the *muscles!*"

117

cuando amarraban a los chuchos con chorizos

Literal meaning: when they tied up
the dogs with sausages

In a nutshell: How long ago was it when grandpa
met grandma? Our iphone calendar doesn't quite
go back that far, so we have to recur to this tall tale.
Come to think of it, though, dogs would probably
love to be tied up with sausages.

"La última vez que vi a tu tío Alfredo todavía
amarraban los chuchos con chorizos." Translation:
"The last time I saw your Uncle Alfredo
I fell off my dinosaur."

OLD GRANDPA SERAPIUS

When an event has occurred in the distant past, another
option is to say it's **del tiempo de Tata Lapo.** This means
that *it is from Grandpa Lapo's time.* Who's the old-timer?
Nineteenth-century military man Serapio Cruz. Now that's
really old!

7

THE BRIGHT SIDE

cabal

In a nutshell: You will hear this term again and again in the country! In generic Spanish **cabal** means *thorough.* But Guatemalans use it in a different sense. "Eran casi las diez y **cabalito** llegó." Translation: "It was almost ten o'clock and he came *right on time.*" On the other hand, if you make a declaration, your friend might reply: **"¡Cabal!"** Here it means: *"Right on!"* When you pay the exact amount of a purchase, the salesperson might respond: **"Cabal tu pisto."** It is as if he's thanking you for exact change. Some make the comment in the exact moment you are counting your change. If so, they mean: *"It's all there."*

calidad

Literal meaning: quality

In a nutshell: If you learn just a few phrases from this book, learn this one! Although this is the standard word for *quality* in all Spanish-speaking countries, here it takes on the sense of *"Cool!"* or *"Awesome!"* For extra credit, don't pronounce the final *d*. It will sound more like **calidá.**

chamusca

Literal meaning: a skirmish

In a nutshell: Soccer is king in Guatemala. And this is the term for the *informal soccer matches* that spontaneously appear in any open area.
"Muchá, ¡a la **chamusca!**"
Translation: "Hey guys, the *soccer game* is on!"

chispudo

Literal meaning: big and sparky

In a nutshell: In most Spanish-speaking countries, if someone is **chispa,** it means he is *bright,* or *clever.* But in Guatemala the form changes to **chispudo.**
"Quizá así comprenderá por qué son tan famosos los chistes del Tío Chema Orellana, un señor ocurrente y **chispudo** que, según cuentan, existió hace mucho."
Translation: "Maybe that way you'll understand why the jokes of Uncle Chema Orellana, a witty and *bright* man who they say lived long ago, are so famous."

chongengue

(pronounced chohn-GEHN-gay)

In a nutshell: *A party.* One economist wrote: "La recesión es la goma después del **chongengue.**"
Translation: "The recession is the hangover after the *party.*"

ganancia

In a nutshell: Ever heard of the baker's dozen? The **ganancia** is essentially the same idea. The next time you go to the market and buy a dozen lemons or oranges, negotiate the price. Then, when they have been packed, say:

"Y ¿la ganancia?"

Your excellent Guatemalan Spanish will bring a smile to the merchant's face, and he will throw in number 13 for free! Just with this tip, you will more than pay for the price of this book!

hoja de pacaya

Literal meaning: pacaya leaf

In a nutshell: When Guatemalans celebrate their traditional festivals, one mainstay is a type of palm branch from the pacaya tree. For that reason, if someone calls you an **hoja de pacaya,** it means you a *party animal* or *social butterfly.* One man who enjoyed posting comments on a local website wrote: "Pareceré **hoja de pacaya** apareciendo en todos los comentarios pero, de verdad, no puedo dejar de decirlo: Es de lo mejor que he leído. Felicitaciones." Translation: "I probably come across as a real *social butterfly* by appearing in almost all the comments, but I can't help but to say: This is the best I have read. Congratulations."

huitecos

Literal meaning: people from Huite

In a nutshell: How many Polacks does it take to change a light bulb? Ten. One to hold the bulb and nine to spin the ladder! Do you remember all those Polack jokes from your childhood? Well, the Guatemalan version comes in the form of **huiteco** jokes. Huite is a small town in the eastern part of the country that has the unfortunate designation of being the country's number one inspiration for punch lines. In fact, one three-member group with a comedic routine call themselves **los tres huitecos.** Their act is essentially a reincarnation of the Three Stooges, Guate-style.

HOW MANY HUITECOS DOES IT TAKE TO...?

Are you ready for a **huiteco** joke? Here's a sample:
¿Cómo sacan los **huitecos** los dólares del país?
¡Los envían por fax y luego destruyen la evidencia!
Translation: How do **huitecos** get dollars out of the country? They send them by fax and then destroy the evidence!

---

estar de peluche

Literal meaning: to be a stuffed animal

How much work has your teddy bear done around the house? Spare me the grizzly details! This cuddly metaphor means *to rest.* "Jamás les he visto trabajar. Se la han pasado **de peluche** toda su vida." Translation: "I have never seen them work. They have lived *the life of Riley.*"

prendérsele el foco

Literal meaning: to turn your flashlight on

In a nutshell: Have you ever had one of those eureka moments? Maybe you were in the middle of taking a shower and the solution to a problem at work came to you in one sudden, intense moment. Whenever that happens, a Guatemalan will instinctively say: **"Se me prendió el foco."** Translation: *"It dawned on me."*

tener leche

Literal meaning: to have milk

In a nutshell: Got milk? If you do, you will do much more than avoid osteoporosis in Guatemala. That's because here milk also means *luck*. Someone lucky is said "to have milk" and can be described as **lechudo,** literally *milky.* "¡Qué **lechudo** este Pedro! Siempre gana en el desmoche." Translation: "Pedro is so *lucky!* He always wins when he plays rummy."

vejiga

Literal meaning: bladder

In a nutshell: Ever had to pee so bad you thought your bladder were going to burst? Of course, usually there is nothing to worry about because your biological tank is up to the task, ready to expand as necessary. A clever Guatemalan saw the similarity with this function and the blowing up of balloons, and a metaphor was born. So ditch the generic Spanish **globo,** and blow up a few **vejigas** for your next party!

"¡Mirá, Elena, todas las **vejigas** son tan chulas!"

Translation: "Elena, look at all the beautiful *balloons!*"

Guatemalan Spanish

8

THE DARK SIDE

agarrarse del chongo

Literal meaning: to grab on to the pony tail

In a nutshell: In Guatemala a **chongo** is a *ponytail.* And when women get violent with each other, it's the first thing they grab. For that reason, **agarrarse del chongo** is the verb form of a *catfight.* "Por celos **se agarraron del chongo** dos mujeres." Translation: "Out of jealousy, two women *got into a catfight.*

bochinche

A public protest or demonstration. "Gane quien gane, habrá **bochinche."** Translation: "No matter who wins, there will be *protests.*"

al bote

Literal meaning: to the boat

In a nutshell: *To jail.* One writer, commenting on the corruption in the justice system, complained: "Bueno, no hay problema, le dan multa de 3,000, un par de años **al bote** y luego a disfrutar de lo robado." Translation: "Well, there's no problem. They get a fine, spend a couple of years **in jail,** and then enjoy what they've stolen." Jail is also referred to as the **tambo.**

casaquero

A liar. "No caigamos en tentaciones de votar por el más **casaquero,** hay que votar por soluciones concretas." Translation: "Let's not fall into the temptation of voting for the biggest *liar.* You've got to vote for concrete solutions." A lie is a **casaca.** (See also **pajero,** page 143.)

Aquí está tu son, Chabela.

Literal meaning: Here's your song, Little Isabel.

In a nutshell: Locally, the nickname for Isabel is **Chabela.** If one of her friends or family members at a dance recognizes one of her favorite tunes, they will nudge her and say: "This one's for you." This, however, has taken on a figurative sense, and if we have been naughty and reap the consequences, this popular saying enters into play. When the government tried to make a deal with a Spanish investor to build a hydroelectric plant in Huehuetenango, hundreds of protesters turned out and the project had to be suspended. Just after a newspaper article describing the events, someone commented: "Resulta que la población, después de tanto palo que ha recibido de tantos gobiernos militares del pasado, ya no cree en [nada].
Aquí está tu son, Chabela."
Translation: "It turns out that the people, after being beaten by so many military governments in the past, no longer believe in [anything]. *What goes around, comes around.*"

bien a mostaza

Literal meaning: well to the mustard

In a nutshell: This is the common term to describe someone who has had one too many drinks. Other variants are **bien abeja, bolo,** and **chara.**
"Casi no logré dormirme anoche porque el vecino estaba **bien a mostaza** e hizo un tremendo alboroto."
Translation: "I almost couldn't get to sleep last night because our neighbor was *really wasted* and was making a big ruckus."

chanchullo

(pronounced chahn-CHUH-yoh)

In a nutshell: *An underhanded business deal* or *cheating of any kind.* In an article about local athletes a journalist wrote: "Son dignos de elogio si se han preparado bien y han competido sin hacer **chanchullo."**
Translation: "They are worthy of praise if they have trained well and competed without *cheating.*"

133

chayes

Literal meaning: broken glass

In a nutshell: This word is yet another gift from the Mayan languages. In the plural form it means *glasses*. "Ponte tus **chayes** para que veas mejor lo que leés." Translation: "Put on your **glasses** so that you can see better what you are reading."

cholero

Literal meaning: house servant, maid

In a nutshell: The **cholero** is a humble domestic servant. But it has also come to mean *in poor taste, low class,* or *rude.* "Los **choleros** corruptos ganaron." Translation: "Those corrupt *scoundrels* won." "Qué **cholero** ese comentario." Translation: "That comment was really *in bad taste.*"

chotear

To spy. "No estoy **choteando** con nadie."
Translation: "I am not *spying* on anyone."

transero

In a nutshell: *An informal street vendor* and a real *wheeler-dealer,* who is always buying and selling something. Unfortunately, in more recent times they have gained notoriety for being *shysters.*
"Prefiero una ama de casa en el Congreso que un viejo mañoso y **transero."**
Translation: "I would prefer a housewife in Congress more than an old, unscrupulous *shyster.*"

con los colochos hechos

Literal meaning: with curls all made up

In a nutshell: The poor girl! She has painstakingly readied herself for a date and tried to look her best. What beautiful curls! But what if the boyfriend never shows? This describes those situations in which we have been *left all dressed up with nowhere to go.*
"A la fiestecita ya no llegó el presidente electo, por lo que me quedé **con los colochos hechos,** porque yo quería presentarme y decirle que puedo ser su mesero exclusivo los próximos cuatro años." Translation: "The president elect never came to the party, and I was *left hanging.* I wanted to introduce myself and tell him I could be his exclusive waiter for the next four years."

BLOW THE WHISTLE!

If an appointment never materializes, tell your Guatemalan friends: 1) **"Me dejaron silbando solo."** Literally, this means: *"They left me whistling to myself."* Or, option 2: **"Quedé chiflando en la loma."** Translation: *"I was left whistling on the hill."*

cuco

A wound. However, it often figuratively refers to a very *sensitive situation* or a *taboo subject.* One headline read: "El **cuco** del aborto." Translation: "The *taboo* of abortion."

El comal le dijo a la olla…

Literal meaning: The tortilla griddle said to the pot…

In a nutshell: Most homes have a **comal,** a *flat griddle* for making tortillas. Many times it shares the stovetop with the **olla,** or *pot.* If one were to give advice to the other, it probably wouldn't be well received. It is the equivalent of *the pot calling the kettle black.* Following an article on political corruption, one man posted: **"El comal le dijo a la olla . . .** ¡Para que se hacen los decentes si todos son ratas de la misma cloaca!" Translation: *"Look who's talking now!* Why do they even pretend to be decent when they are all rats from the same sewer!"

deschongue

An uproar or *chaos.* When a local highway was bottlenecked due to construction, one man wrote: "Tuve la oportunidad de ser parte del **deschongue** que se formó en la carretera." Translation: "I had the [unfortunate] chance to be part of the *complete mess* that formed on the highway."

irse de capiuza

To play hookie. "Roberto reprobó el quinto grado porque la mitad del año **se iba de capiuza.**" Translation: "Roberto failed fifth grade because he spent half the year *playing hookie.*"

en capilla ardiente

Literal meaning: in a burning chapel

In a nutshell: Imagine the scene: A loved one has been condemned to death and will be executed the following day. A vigil is held where it is "burning" inside the chapel in the sense that many candles are lit. Those present wonder what will happen to the offender. For this reason, to be **en capilla ardiente** means to be *in suspense, awaiting some negative consequence.* It is similar to *waiting for the other shoe to drop,* but more ominous. "Un hombre de 21 años permaneció **en capilla ardiente** ayer tras ser capturado por una turba de vecinos que pretendía lincharlo debido a que había robado una motocicleta." Translation: "A 21-year-old man who had stolen a motorcycle suddenly found himself *in hot water [as to his fate]* yesterday after being captured by a mob of neighbors who nearly lynched him."

La pita se revienta por lo angosto.

Literal meaning: The cord snaps in its thinnest part.

In a nutshell: When a corrupt military official was arrested, one man blogged: "El problema es que […] **la pita se rompe por lo angosto.** Esta persona, antes de ser extraditado a su país, debería ser interrogado para que declare de donde venían sus órdenes y enviar copia de su testimonio a un tribunal internacional."

Translation: "The problem is that *a chain is only as strong as its weakest link.* This person, before being extradited to his country, should have been interrogated so as to reveal where his orders came from and to send his testimony to an international court." (See also **pitiar,** page 51.)

llamaradas de tusas

Literal meaning: flames of the corn leaves

In a nutshell: Locally the leaves of the corn plant are called **tusas.** When they dry out, they are great for starting fires because they will catch blaze almost immediately. On the other hand, their delicate design can't sustain combustion for more than a few minutes. So when natives say that something is just a **llamarada de tusa,** they are talking about *a short-lived enthusiasm* or *happiness.* When 18 judges were recently indicted for abuse of power, one reader posted: "Hay que sentar un precedente con todos estos jueces, de lo contrario solo será una **llamarada de tusas."** Translation: "We have to set a precedent with all these judges. Otherwise, it will be just be *a flash in the pan.*"

llevarse de corbata

Literal meaning: to take by the necktie

To implicate or *frame*. "Hay fiscales capaces de plantar evidencia para **llevarse de corbata** a cualquier incauto con cara de chivo expiatorio." Translation: "There are district attorneys capable of planting evidence *to implicate* any unwary soul as a scapegoat."

molonquear

To beat with the fists. "Cuando rehusé compartir mis champurradas con mi hermano, me dio una buena **molonqueada.**" Translation: "When I refused to share my cookies with my brother, he gave me a good *beating.*"

ñañaras

(Pronounced YAHN-yah-rahs)

Goosebumps. "Sentí **ñañaras** caminando por el cementerio de noche." Translation: "It gave me the *heebie-jeebies* to walk through the cemetery at night."

pajero

In a nutshell: Down on the farm there's lots of straw for the animals. But just one straw doesn't hold up well in the wind, and it is easily blown away. Figuratively, then, **paja** has come to mean something even more flimsy: *a lie.* "No seas **pajero.** Decíle a tu mamá la verdad." Translation: "Don't be a *liar.* Tell your mother the truth."

pashtudo

In a nutshell: A **pashte** is a dried fruit that is used as a natural defoliator when you take a shower. But if someone is said to be **pashtudo,** he probably hasn't cared much about his appearance. It refers to *a person with mangled hair.* "Manuelito, no andes platicando con todos esos **pashtudos** allá en el parque." Translation: "Manuelito, don't go talking to all those *hippies* down at the park."

quemarse

Literal meaning: to get burned

To incriminate oneself, to give oneself away. "No sabíamos quién había roto la macetera, hasta que Julio, riéndose, **se quemó.**" Translation: "We didn't know who had broken the pot until Julio, laughing, *gave himself away.*" (See **darse color,** page 157.)

petatear

In a nutshell: *To die.* In ancient Mayan culture, the dead were laid to rest wrapped in a **petate,** a type of *natural-fiber rug* that could even be used as a sleeping mat. The Guatemalans have converted the word into a verb and it has become a euphemism for *dying.*

"Don Julio ya **petatió."**

Translation: "Don Julio already *kicked the bucket.*"

TAKING ADVANTAGE

The **petate** functions as a most primitive sleeping mat, and is graciously offered to overnight guests. But apparently some who accepted such hospitality abused the host's kindness. So the phrase **de a petate** has taken on the meaning of *taking advantage of others.* "Qué **de a petate,** es fácil solo pedir." Translation: *"What ingratitude!* It is easy just to ask for more and more."

quedar sin el mico y sin la montera

Literal meaning: to be left without the monkey and without the saddle

In a nutshell: In the rurals some have monkeys, or **micos,** as pets. And every cowboy values his saddle, or **montera.** But when things go wrong, he stands to lose everything. And all for a little monkey business! After a presidential divorce some years ago, one reader wrote: "Uy, ¡qué feo estar en el pellejo de Sandrita Torres, pues de la noche a la mañana se puede **quedar sin el mico y sin la montera,** sin su gavilán y sin su apetecida guayaba!"
Translation: "How terrible it would be to trade places with Sandrita Torres because overnight she could be *left with nothing,* without her husband and without her cushy government job!"

A MOST DESIRABLE FRUIT

As you may have noticed in the example above, a **guayaba** is much more than a fruit. Figuratively, it refers to *a comfortable job in high places,* generally within the government. Sweet!

Si no es crudo, es quemado.

Literal meaning: If it's not raw, it's burnt.

In a nutshell: Nothing is ever perfect in life. Try this: The next time something unpleasant happens, just offer this local saying with a sigh. It's akin to: *"If it's not one thing, it's another."*

ver la cosa peluda

Literal meaning: see the thing hairy

In a nutshell: Sometimes hairy is scary! So if someone sees a matter as hairy, it means he is *realizing the magnitude of a difficult situation.* "Cuando sus acreedores comenzaron a llamarle a Juan diariamente, el pobrecito comenzó a **ver la cosa peluda."** Translation: "When Juan's creditors began calling him daily, the poor guy began *to see the handwriting on the wall.*"

Unos en la pena, y otros en la pepena.

Literal meaning: Some in sorrow, and others picking and choosing.

In a nutshell: When tragedy strikes, there are often two reactions. On the one hand, it can bring out the best in some who react with true compassion. But conversely, there are also those who are only interested in taking advantage of the situation. This saying suggests that while some are mourning **(pena),** others dedicate themselves to the **pepena.** The verb **pepenar** has its roots in the Nahuatl language and means *to pick and choose amongst several items.*

When an earthquake recently hit the country, this saying was the headline of an opinion piece exposing how some leaders were making undue profit from the relief efforts. Whenever price gouging and looting arise after natural disasters, this is the adage of choice.

9

A LITTLE
PERSONALITY

aguambado

Slow to think, foolish. "El pobre patajo era tan **aguambado** que ni siquiera pudo hacer bien un simple mandado." Translation: "The poor boy was so *dumb* he couldn't even run a simple errand."

canela fina

Literal meaning: fine cinnamon

Cinnamon sticks are extremely brittle. It doesn't take much for them to crumble under the least of pressure. Similarly, *a person who is easily offended* is likened to this fragile condiment. "Invítale también a la Irene. Ya sabés que es **canela fina.**" Translation: "Remember to invite Irene. You know how *sensitive* she is." In other contexts **canela fina** refers to *a difficult problem.*

canche

In a nutshell: *A light-skinned person.* You will find that Guatemalans are generally less conscious of skin color than their English-speaking counterparts. If you are of light complexion, you may hear someone tell you in the market: "¿Qué le damos, **canchito?"** Translation: "What can we get for you, *whitey?"* But relax! This usually has no racial connotations. Rather, it is practically a term of endearment, and the seller is just trying to butter you up. On the other hand, since most foreigners are of lighter complexion than the locals, **canche** is sometimes applied to anyone from abroad, similar to **gringo.** (See also **grencho,** page 158.)

THE WHITE SLEEP

In Nicaragua, Honduras, and El Salvador light-skinned people are called **cheles.** In Guatemala, though, **cheles** has taken on a peculiar meaning: *the sleep in your eyes!* One man wrote: "El pobre Fajardo ni los **cheles** de tanto llorar se limpió en la conferencia." Translation: "Poor Fajardo, even with so much crying, couldn't wipe the *sleep* from his eyes." In other contexts, **cheles** can mean *fear.*

caquero

Literal meaning: filled with excrement

In a nutshell: *Stuck-up.* The Spanish word for *poop* is **caca**. To describe someone who thinks too much of himself, we might say in English: "He's full of it!" This Guatemalan adjective carries the same idea. Often it is applied to persons who have come into money and flaunt it. "Ahora que Orlando tiene su negocio, se ha vuelto todo **caquero.** Ni me habla." Translation: "Now that Orlando has his own business, he's *full of it.* He doesn't even talk to me anymore."

catrín

To be well dressed. "Katia va bien **catrín** al chongengue."
Translation: "Katia is going *dressed to a tee* to the party."

152

chapín

In a nutshell: Nickname for *Guatemalan*. Why are Guatemalans called **chapines?** There is no definitive answer. But here are at least three theories: 1) Some say that those who lived in outlying areas of the country used to call the inhabitants of the capital **chapines,** in reference to a type of ornate shoe worn there. 2) Another hypothesis is that **chapín** comes from the name of the southernmost state in Mexico, called Chiapas. And 3) it may be a derivation of the French word *chapeau*, a kind of hat that locals may have worn.

chusema

Someone not right in the head, a nutcase. "Mejor no le hagás caso a ese viejo **chusema."** Translation: "You better not pay attention to that *crazy old man*."

chevo

Literal meaning: Little Eusebius

In a nutshell: *Foolish.* In her *Diccionario de jergas de habla hispana,* Roxanna Fitch relates that in Quetzaltenango there lived a certain unfortunate fellow named Eusebio. For short, they called him **Chevo.** Sadly, poor Mr. Chevo wasn't very bright. They invited him to a party, but when the day came, it was raining heavily. Unable to phone, he went to the party site and in the threshold announced: "I just came to let you know I am not going to make it because it's raining so hard."
"Me pregunto que se puede esperar cuando un **chevo** aconseja a otro **chevo.**"
Translation: "I wonder what can happen when one *fool* gives advice to another."
The word can also be used as an adjective.
"No seas **chevo.**"
Translation: "Don't be *silly.*"
Try this: If you see someone do something truly foolish, just say: **"¡Ah, don Chevo!"** It's like saying sarcastically: *"Boy, aren't you smart!"*

choca

Literal meaning: crash

In a nutshell: Check out the back cover of this book. The coin you see there is a 25-cent piece, known as a **choca.** Why **choca?** Guatemalans also call those who are blind **chocos.** On the coin only the profile of the woman is pictured, revealing only one squinty eye. So people jokingly began to call her **choca,** or *blind.* This second sense is used frequently in everyday speech, especially if someone bumps into something because of not paying attention. "¡Tan **choco** que sos!" Translation: "Hey, are you *blind?*" The implication is: Pay attention and watch where you are going!

155

choya

(pronounced CHOH-yah)

Literal meaning: understanding, judgment, head

In a nutshell: In most areas of Guatemala, people are not in as much of a hurry as their North American counterparts. So be patient and get ready to wait! But if a friend of yours is going excessively slow, use this phrase: "¡Con que **choya** vas!" Translation: "Man, you are really going *slow!*" The implication is to get a move on! In other contexts it takes on the sense of *laziness*. One headline read: "A mí también me entró la **choya** del fin de año." Translation: "I also got caught up in the end-of-year *laziness*." The adjective form is **choyudo.**

cusco

(pronounced KOO-skoh)

Flirtatious. "Qué **cusca** es Lorena." Translation: "Lorena is such a *flirt.*"

dar color

To discover someone's true colors or character. "Ella **da color** públicamente apoyando a un militar de los que ella ha dicho que se supone son sus enemigos." Translation: "She *shows her true colors* publicly by supporting a military man who she supposedly said is her enemy."

On the other hand, **darse color** can mean *to give oneself away.* "Puede ser que no llevaban ni un centavo, ni para la gasolina, para no **darse color.**" Translation: "It may be that he didn't have even a penny on him for gasoline so as to not *give himself away.*"

fufurufo
(pronounced foo-foo-ROO-foh)

Stuck-up, high class. "María anda bien **fufurufa** con sus nuevos tacones." Translation: "María is walking around *all uppity* with her new high heels."

grencho

In a nutshell: *American.* Just before a soccer match between Guatemala and the United States, one man posted the following: "¡Ánimo, muchachos, hay que ganarle a los **grenchos** y a todo el que se ponga enfrente! No olviden que el fútbol es colectivo." Translation: "Come on, boys! Let's beat the *Americans* and whatever they throw at us! Don't forget that soccer is a team sport."

La vida de chancle es cara, pero la otra no es vida.

Literal meaning: The life of the vain is expensive, but the other option isn't life.

In a nutshell: A **chancle** is a person who is *conceited.* "Mientras nosotros no entendamos eso, la pobreza seguirá siendo un mal endémico en Guatemala. Como dice el refrán: **'La vida de chancle es cara… pero la otra no es vida.'** Los ricos se pueden dar muchos lujos; los pobres, no." Translation: "As long as we don't understand that, poverty will continue to be endemic to Guatemala. As the sayings goes: *'The life of the privileged is expensive, but the other alternative is no life at all.'* The rich can afford their luxuries, but the poor cannot."

pichicato

Tight-fisted, miserly. "Mi tío es bien **pichicato.** Nunca nos regala nada." Translation: "My uncle is really *stingy.* He never gives us any presents." Such a person can also be described as **codo, tacaño** or **agarrado.**

ponerse buzo

Literal meaning: to become a diver

In a nutshell: A **buzo** is a diver. When at deep sea and dependent on his oxygen supply, he can't afford to be careless. So when someone tells you **"ponéte buzo,"** he means *"be alert."*
"Si vas a ir a la Zona 18, **¡ponéte buzo!"** Translation: "If you are going into Zone 18, *keep your eyes wide open!"*

quishpinudo

In a nutshell: Ever had a bad hair day? If so, your heart will go out to all the **quishpinudos.** Why? Because this is the adjective to describe *hair that stands on end.* "¿No conocés a Rodrigo? Es el vecino **quishpinudo** que vive en frente?" Translation: "Don't you know Rodrigo? He's the neighbor across the street, the guy *whose hair stands straight up.*"

recachureco

In a nutshell: When do we stop being fans and become fanatics? **Cachureco** is a term coined by General Justo Rufino Barrios to refer to very conservative Catholics. In Spanish, the prefix *re* intensifies the action, so **recachureco** means *fanatical,* and refers to *those who blindly follow a religion.* "Cada Semana Santa muy de madrugada yo te tomaba fotos, porque eras buen devoto cargador **recachureco."** Translation: "Every Holy Week early in the morning I snapped pictures of you, because you were a devout, fanatical bearer [of images].

Se topó la piedra con el coyol.

Literal meaning: The rock has met the tough-skinned fruit.

In a nutshell: The **coyol** is a small, round fruit with a skin that is quite difficult to break. So when someone says, **"Se topó la piedra con el coyol,"** it means: *"He has met his match."* This especially applies when a person with a difficult personality runs into someone even more difficult to deal with. I don't know about you, but I'm getting out of here!

shute

In a nutshell: Ever heard of rubbernecking delays? That's what happens when, because of perhaps a simple fender bender, the flow of traffic comes nearly to a halt, just so all the curious can get a gander at what happened. If you are a rubbernecker or a buttinsky, don't be surprised if in Guatemala you are described as **shute,** which essentially means *nosy, prying* or *snoopy,* and not of the Charlie Brown variety!

Originally, **shute** was used to designate a *stinger,* such as those used by bees and wasps to pierce our skin. The nosy person similarly sticks his nose in where it doesn't belong and causes great figurative pain. "A nuestro vicepresidente le encanta recibir palo. Al menos esa es la lectura que yo le doy el querer sacar la cara para comunicar el aumento de salarios en un momento más impertinente que una suegra **shute** en la luna de miel." Translation: "Our vice president loves to get beat up. At least that's what I read into the fact that he shows his face to communicate a salary increase at a moment more awkward than having a *nosy* mother-in-law along for the honeymoon." Yikes!

Si querés, mejor te llevo al Registro.

Literal meaning: If you like,
I better take you to the Public Registry.

In a nutshell: Give someone an inch and he wants
to take a yard. How do you put those greedy people
in their place? Try this Guatemalan saying to put an
end to being taken advantage of. Since the Public
Registry is where you go to adopt someone, the
implied idea is that the person is taking so much
from you, he or she might as well be your child!

THE YOLK'S ON THEM!

Try this one on the next pushy person who tries to take advantage of you. Just say: **"¿Y no querés pan con pollo?"** This literally means, *"And don't you want bread with chicken?"* In reality, the yolk will be on them, so to speak, because this is a common way of making listeners come back down to Earth and have realistic expectations. It's kind of like saying, *"You can't have your cake and eat it, too."* A shortened form is **"Y, ¿pollo no querés?"**

talishte

In a nutshell: *Tough, resistant,* or *persistent.*
One blogger wrote: "Así que, como dicen
aquí en nuestra tierra, hay que ser **talishte**
para alcanzar lo que siempre hemos soñado."
Translation: "So as they say in our country,
you've got to be *tough* to make your dreams
come true." On the other hand, with
inanimate objects, it means *resistant.*
"¡Qué **talishtes** tus zapatos vos!"
Translation: "Man, those shoes are really
durable!"

trompudo

Literal meaning: big-lipped

In a nutshell: Someone that has *enlarged lips* could be described in Spanish as **trompudo** (not exactly a compliment). Since people tend to pout when they are unhappy about something, Guatemalans have taken it to mean *annoyed,* or *angry.* "El presidente Colom se puso **trompudo** porque, según él, los medios escritos boicoteaban su programa de Cohesión Social."

Translation: "President Colom got *annoyed* because, according to him, the print media boycotted his Social Cohesion program." Recently, the government urged the public to get their new personal identification cards. In order to encourage compliance, large billboards warned: "Si después no le cambian el cheque, no se vaya a poner **trompudo."** Translation: "If later they don't want to cash your check, don't *get mad.*"

10

THE GOLDEN GANANCIA

¿Creés que vengo de arrear pijijes?

Literal meaning: Do you think I am coming from shepherding wild ducks?

In a nutshell: Pijijes (pronounced pee-HEE-hays) are *wild ducks* that by nature are impossible to guide. Only a fool would even try to round them up.
"Es que los politiqueros de este país creen que todavía venimos **de arrear pijijes.**"
Translation: "This country's politicians think that *we were born yesterday.*"
Congratulations! You are now the proud possessor of more than 200 key Guatemalan words, phrases and sayings. Regardless of how many **pijijes** you may have rounded up in the past, as you practice your newfound portfolio, no one will take you for someone born yesterday! So put that **shola** to work!

*Forgot what a **ganancia** is? Go back to page 123.*

gringoguide2OO

Guatemalan Spanish

INDEX

A

A cada coche le llega
   su sábado **104**
achimero **56**
acuchuchar **38**
A ése no le gana una olla
   de tamales **96**
agarrarse del chongo **130**
agua **87**
agua entubada **87**
aguambado **150**
agua pura **87**
¡Aguas! **15**
alagartado **81**
¡A la gran! **14**
alboroto **88**
al bote **131**
amishado **117**
¡Aprovéchate Matías, que esto no
   es de todos los días! **12**, **82**
Aquí está tu son, Chabela **132**
arce, Me agarraste de tu **68**

arrastrado **60**
atol **85**
A veces el pato nada, y a
   veces ni agua toma **105**

B

barajearla más despacio **21**
Barrios, General Justo Rufino **161**
bien **21**
bien a mostaza **133**
bish, hacer **98**
boca chiquita, hacerse de la **86**
bochinche **130**
bolas, andan las **65**
bola, se regó la **65**
bote, al **131**
¡Brincos dieras! **22**
brocha **107**
buitrear **106**
bultos **34**
burra **23**, **107**

W

wisa **54**

Z

¡Ya son las doce, y la gal-
   lina no se coce! **80**
¡Ydiay! **18**
¿Y no querés pan con pollo? **164**
yuca **94**

Z

zanates **113**

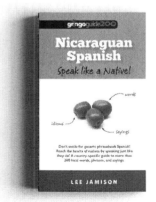
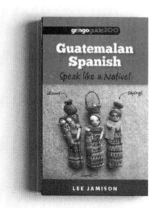

Made in the USA
Columbia, SC
09 July 2020

13513453R00098